GREAT PETS

Hamsters and Gerbils

Carol Ellis

 Marshall Cavendish
Benchmark

New York

Marshall Cavendish Benchmark
99 White Plains Road
Tarrytown, New York 10591
www.marshallcavendish.us

Library of Congress Cataloging-in-Publication Data
Ellis, Carol, date
Hamsters and gerbils / by Carol Ellis.
p. cm. -- (Great pets)
Includes bibliographical references and index.
Summary: "Describes the characteristics and behavior of pet hamsters and
gerbils, also discussing their physical appearance and place in
history"--Provided by publisher.
ISBN 978-0-7614-2999-9
1. Hamsters as pets--Juvenile literature. 2. Gerbils as pets--Juvenile
literature. I. Title.
SF459.H3E45 2009
636.935'6--dc22
2008024336

Front cover: Gerbils
Title page: Two Roborovski hamsters
Back cover: A golden, or Syrian, hamster

Photo research by Candlepants, Inc.
Front Cover: Maximilian Weinzierl / Alamy
The photographs in this book are used by permission and through the courtesy of:
Alamy: Iaian Cooper, 1, 39; Maximilian Weinzierl, 4, 10, 20, 30; Les Gibbon, 7, 9, 27; Juniors Bildarchiv, 14, 16, 29;
Petra Wegner, 19, 31; Papillo, 21; Michael Krabs, 22; onderlandstock, 26; MasPix, 34; Robert Pickett, 36. Photo
Researchers: Toni Angermayer, back cover; Stuart Wilson, 13; Ray Coleman, 24; Jerome Wexler, 32. Peter Arnold, Inc.:
WILDLIFE, 6; BIOSPHOTO / J.L. Klein & M. L. Hubert, 15; C. Steimer, 18, 40; BIOSPHOTO / Michel Gunther, 41.
Animals Animals / Earth Scenes: ULRIKE SCHANZ, 8. Minden Pictures: Heidi & Hans-Jurgen Koch, 28.

Editor: Karen Ang
Publisher: Michelle Bisson
Art Director: Anahid Hamparian
Series Design by: Elynn Cohen

Printed in Malaysia
6 5 4 3 2 1

Contents

1

Little Friends

With their bright eyes and curious nature, hamsters and gerbils have burrowed their way into the hearts of pet lovers all over the world. Take a walk through a large pet store, and somewhere among the bird cages and the tropical fish tanks, you are almost sure to find a display of these cute, furry animals. You will see them at pet shows, on Web sites, in books, and even on television shows.

One reason why people like these animals so much is because they are small and pretty easy to care for. Their size makes them ideal pets for people who live in apartments or small houses. They do not need leashes, long walks, or litter boxes. Even more importantly, they are great fun to watch as they go through their busy routines of digging, nesting, and playing. Once they get to know you, most pet hamsters and gerbils will treat you like a very big friend.

Small pets like hamsters and gerbils are very popular because of their size, how easy they are to care for, and their friendly personalities.

In the wild, hamsters eat seeds, grasses, and vegetables, and live in burrows underground.

The Path to Pethood

It was not until the twentieth century that many people began keeping hamsters and gerbils as pets. Long before that, many people thought of them as pests because they ate the crops farmers had planted. One type of wild hamster can store more than one hundred pounds of food in its underground burrow!

Not everyone thought hamsters and gerbils were pests. Scientists who were trying to discover cures for diseases knew they could learn a lot by

A gerbil family huddles together for security and warmth.

studying the animals in their laboratories. One of those scientists, Dr. Saul Adler, wanted to study hamsters. His friend, Professor Israel Aharoni of the University of Jerusalem, traveled to the Middle Eastern country of Syria in 1930. With the help of a local guide, he found a mother hamster and eleven **pups**—or baby hamsters—curled in their nest eight feet beneath the ground. Some of them escaped when he took them back to Jerusalem, but eventually, one of the females had babies. Professor Aharoni gave some to Dr. Adler, and when they had pups, Dr. Adler began giving them to scientists in other countries. In 1938, the first Syrian hamsters arrived in the United States.

Like hamsters, gerbils were first kept as laboratory animals. In 1935, forty gerbils were captured in the Asian country of Mongolia and sent to Japan for research purposes. The **descendants** of these gerbils arrived in the United States.

One reason why hamsters and gerbils were easy to study in the laboratories was becuase they did not require a lot of space. This trait also makes them good pets for people who do not want larger animals.

It is a lot of fun to watch gerbils as they go about their daily activities.

As they studied the hamsters and gerbils, many scientists grew to enjoy the curious, friendly creatures. They liked them so much that they began taking some of them into their homes for themselves and for their children to keep. The scientists had discovered what so many people know today—these little animals make great pets!

2

Hamster or Gerbil?

If you are thinking of getting a hamster or a gerbil, it is a good idea to know what makes them alike and what makes them different. Hamsters and gerbils are both **rodents,** like mice, guinea pigs, chipmunks, and many other small animals. The word rodent comes from the Latin word, *rodere,* which means "to **gnaw.**" Like all rodents, hamsters and gerbils have strong front teeth called **incisors.** They can chew through cardboard, wood, and even hard plastic.

Both gerbils and hamsters are diggers, too. In the wild, they burrow underground where they are safe from **predators,** such as owls, eagles, and desert foxes. Hamsters and gerbils can cover a lot of territory, digging long tunnels and building different chambers for sleeping, storing food, going to the bathroom, and having pups.

One of the most obvious differences between gerbils and hamsters is their tails. Most hamsters have very short—or almost no—tails. Gerbils have long tails that are sometimes as long as their bodies.

HAMSTER AND GERBIL FACTS

	Hamsters	Gerbils
Lifespan:	2 to 3 years	3 to 5 years
Length:	2 to 7 inches (5 to 17.8 centimeters)	4 to 5 inches (10.2 to 12.7 cm) plus a tail of about the same length
Habits:	Sleep during most of the day and become active at night.	Active several times throughout the day and night.

When deciding between hamsters and gerbils, one of the most important things to know is that the most common pet hamster—the Syrian hamster or golden hamster—is a solitary little animal. That means that it should be housed alone because it will fight fiercely with other hamsters. But a pet Syrian hamster is almost always friendly and good-natured with its humans.

Unlike the Syrian hamster, a gerbil might be miserable living alone. Gerbils like to groom each other's fur and often sleep curled up together. To feel safe and be happy, a pet gerbil needs to live with at least one other gerbil. However, it is best if they come from the same litter or have lived together since they were very young. Keeping two older gerbils that have never seen each other before may cause fighting. It is also important to make sure that you get either two males or two females. If you get one male and one female, you will most likely end up with too many gerbil babies.

Where to Get Your Pet

When you have decided which pet is right for you, it is time to find one. The best place to get your hamster or gerbils is from a local **breeder.** Most breeders take care to keep their animals healthy. They usually spend time handling them so they are not afraid of human contact. A breeder should be able to answer all the questions you will have about caring for your new pet.

Another good place to look is a local animal shelter or a pet rescue organization. These groups take in abandoned animals and make sure that they are healthy before they place them in good homes. You can find breeders, rescue organizations, and animal shelters in the telephone book and on the Internet.

Never buy a hamster or gerbil that is very young. Responsible breeders or pet stores will not sell the animals until they are ready for new homes.

Most people purchase hamsters and gerbils at pet stores. Many pet stores sell different breeds, or types, of hamsters and gerbils.

Picking the Right Pet

No matter where you get your pet, it is important to spend some time watching the animals to see if they look healthy. Are the animal's eyes bright and shiny? Does its fur look soft and clean? Do its ears and nose look crusty or dirty? Does it seem to move around, or does it just sit still and not interact with anything around it? (Since hamsters are nocturnal, you should try to visit during the evening when they are active.)

The place where you are getting your pet is also important. Does it seem like the people selling you the animal are knowledgeable? Does the area where the hamsters or gerbils are kept look clean? Are there plenty of food, water, and hiding places available to the animals? Is there enough

Hamsters and gerbils that are alert and active are usually healthy. Just be sure to look at the animals at the time of day or night when they are supposed to be active.

space in the cages or tanks for the animals? If the answer to most of these question is "no" then you should not get your pet from that place. If the animals look sick or the place where they live looks dirty, you will most likely bring home a sick pet. Also, you do not want to give your business to people or stores that do not take proper care of their animals.

It is important to watch how the animals interact with each other. If the one you want seems to be fighting with others, you should probably pick a different one.

If the animals look healthy, and the living space looks clean, ask to hold some of them. You need to make sure that the pet you bring home will be comfortable with being held. Most hamsters and gerbils will be a little nervous at first. But if after some gentle holding or petting the animal does not calm down, you might want to select a different one. Do not be afraid to ask the breeder, rescuer, or store worker about the animals. Some questions might be how old the animals are, how long they have been there, are some more—or less—friendly than others. Asking the right questions and making a careful decision can help you to bring home the perfect little friend.

3

Types of Hamsters and Gerbils

There are many **species** of hamsters living in the wild, but only a few types have become pets. This is because of their size, their personalities, and how easy it is to care for them. Here is a list of some of the most popular hamster breeds.

Syrian Hamsters

The Syrian, or golden, hamster is the one type most often kept as a pet. It is the largest of the pet hamsters and grows to be about 7 inches (17.8 cm) long. It has a barrel-shaped body and almost no tail. Nearly all pet Syrian hamsters are descended from the ones captured by Professor Aharoni in 1930.

A dwarf Chinese hamster peeks out from a houseplant. Always be sure that your hamster or gerbil does not chew on or eat houseplants because those plants could be poisonous.

The Syrian is often called the golden hamster because the species originally had golden brown fur. Today, the Syrian hamster comes in many other colors such as black, cinnamon, cream, and gray. It can also have fur that is patterned—-with one main color and spots or bands of another color.

Pet Syrian hamsters also come in a variety of coat-types. A satin coat is glossy, while the velvety rex coat can be long and wavy or short and curly. A short-haired Syrian rex even has curly whiskers. Syrian teddy bear hamsters have long hair that you can brush with a soft toothbrush or a small brush made for small animals.

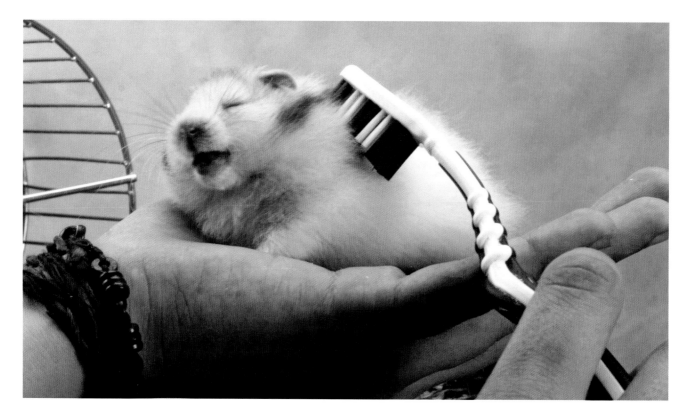

This golden hamster enjoys having its coat gently brushed with a toothbrush.

Dwarf Hamsters

Another species of hamster that has become popular as a pet is the dwarf hamster. Dwarf hamsters are smaller than Syrian hamsters. They live in pairs or groups in the wild, and can often—but not always—share a cage if they start together at a very young age.

In the wild, the dwarf Campbell's Russian hamster lives in the deserts and sand dunes of Mongolia and China. The Campbell's Russian is about 4 inches (10.2 cm) long, and has a thick shiny coat that covers even its feet. Sometimes this is called the "furry-footed hamster." This hamster's most common color is its original one—brownish-gray on top with a cream-colored stomach. However, you can also find it in other colors, including blue-gray, pure white, and an orange-type color.

The dwarf winter white Russian hamster is about 3 inches (7.6 cm) long. It comes from parts of northern Asia and Siberia, and is often called the Siberian hamster. It has gray fur that may turn pure white in the winter. Like its close relative, the Campbell's Russian hamster, the winter white is usually friendly and easy to tame.

Siberian hamsters are very popular pets because of their size and friendliness.

In the wild, the dwarf Chinese hamster is found in Northern China and Mongolia. It is about 4 inches (10.2 cm) long and looks a little like a mouse, with a longer tail and a thinner body than most other pet hamsters. Its coat comes in two varieties—brown with a dark stripe down the center of the back and a white stomach, or white with brown patches.

The Roborovski hamster is a tiny creature from Mongolia. It is only about 2 inches (5 cm) long. It is one of the newest hamster species to be kept as a pet. This hamster has a sandy-colored coat and white "eyebrows." Lively and very fast on its feet, the Roborovski is wriggly and not easy to handle.

Roborovski hamsters are small enough to easily use toilet paper and paper towel tubes as burrows.

A Hamster's Cheeks

Hamster comes from the German word *hamstern*, meaning "to hoard." Hamsters are famous for gathering and hiding huge amounts of food. To get the food back to their nests, they use their cheek pouches the way people use grocery bags. A hamster's cheek pouches can stretch out to hold almost half the hamster's weight in food!

Many owners, however, think that it is a lot of fun to watch. This is especially true if it has a large cage with plenty of room to run and play.

Gerbils

There are many more species of wild gerbils than of hamsters, but most pet gerbils are descended from the forty that were captured in Mongolia in 1935. The Mongolian gerbil is bigger than a mouse, but smaller than most hamsters. Gerbils can range in size from 4 to 5 inches.

Gerbils have big bright eyes and small ears. A gerbil uses its long muscular hind legs to jump, and will stand up on them to sniff the air and check out its surroundings. In the wild, gerbils warn each other of danger by thumping their hind feet. If something frightens your pet gerbils, you might see and hear

Using their back legs and tails to balance, these gerbils stand up to check out their surroundings.

them thumping. A gerbil's furry tail is usually as long as its body. Some gerbils have a tuft of fur on the end of the tail.

In the past, nearly all pet gerbils were a sandy brown color with a white stomach and a black band on the back. Today, you can find pet gerbils in many colors, including golden, cinnamon, dove gray, apricot, and white.

Choosing among the many different coats and colors is part of the fun of finding a hamster or a gerbil. But whether your new pet is a black teddy-bear hamster or a couple of cinnamon-colored gerbils, the most fun will be getting to know and love it.

GERBIL TAILS

A gerbil's tail helps it stay balanced when it sits up on its back legs. The tail is useful in another way, too. If a wild gerbil is caught by its tail and cannot escape from a predator, such as an owl, part of its tail will come off, and the bird is left holding almost nothing but fur! Your pet gerbil's tail might break off just like a wild gerbil's, so be sure not to pick it up by its tail.

4

At Home with Your New Pet

Hamsters and gerbils are sometimes called pocket pets because they are small enough to fit into your pocket. But both little animals are born with the instinct to do all the things their ancestors did in the wild. They dig, build nests, gnaw, store food, and run around. You will want to give them a place that is big enough and safe enough for these activities.

Your Pet's Home

A glass aquarium—at least 10-gallon (37.9-liter) tank—makes a good home for a Syrian hamster or a couple of gerbils. It should have a wire mesh cover that fits over the top. This allows plenty of air into the tank, and also keeps your pet in and other pets out. You could also use a wire cage if the bars are close

Some hamsters enjoy hiding out and riding around in pockets.

enough together to keep your pet from squeezing between them. Dwarf hamsters are small enough to squeeze between most bars, so they should be kept in an aquarium. Cages made especially for hamsters or gerbils are sold in many pet stores. Some are wire, while others are made of plastic with built-in tubes, platforms, and tunnels. Make sure the tubes and tunnels are wide enough for your pets and that they are securely connected to the rest of the cage. With plastic cages, you should frequently check to make sure your pet has not chewed through the plastic.

Some cages come with many different parts for your hamster or gerbil to explore and hide in. Always make sure, however, that there is no way for your pet to escape from its cage.

Always make sure that your pet's cage is safe from other household pets.

Keep your pet's cage in a quiet place where it will not get too cold or too hot. Inside the cage, cover the floor of the cage with plenty of bedding for your pet to tunnel and burrow in. You should use aspen wood shavings or paper bedding that is sold in pet stores. Many breeders and experienced hamster and gerbil owners do not recommend using cedar or pine shavings because those can make your pet sick.

Both hamsters and gerbils need to arrange their homes, just as their wild relatives do. If you give them strips of clean, white, unscented toilet paper, they will shred it and build sleeping nests with it. A wooden box or a ceramic or plastic house will give them a feeling of safety when they curl up inside.

A hamster's or gerbil's teeth never stop growing. To keep their teeth from getting too long, your pet has to chew—a lot. At pet stores, you can find wooden chew sticks and blocks made especially for hamsters and gerbils. You can also give them empty paper towel and toilet paper rolls. Not only will they chew and shred them, but they can even use the rolls as tunnels. Never give your hamster or gerbil chew toys made for cats, dogs, or other animals. Certain materials, paints, and dyes that are not harmful to these larger animals can be deadly to hamsters and gerbils.

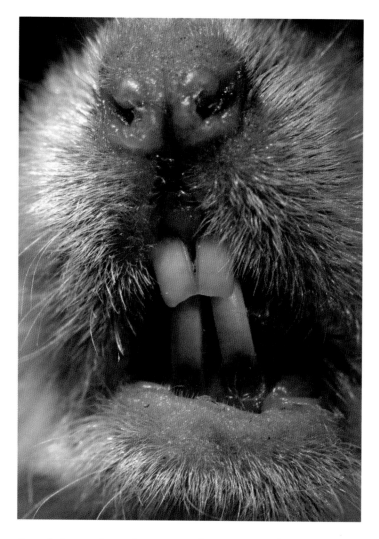

Special wooden chew toys that are made just for hamsters and gerbils will help to keep their teeth at the right length.

Food and Water

The best way to make sure your pets get a good diet is to feed them a gerbil or hamster mix that you can buy at the pet store. The seeds, grains, and nuts will give them almost all the nutrition they need. You should also offer tasty bits of fresh strawberries or carrots. Both hamsters and gerbils love sunflower

A mix of store-bought hamster or gerbil food and some fresh fruits and vegetables will help your pet stay healthy.

seeds, but too many seeds will make them fat and unhealthy. Save the seeds for a special treat. Some foods, such as chocolate and lettuce, can be unhealthy or even poisonous for your pet. You can check with a veterinarian, breeder, pet store worker, or on the Internet for a list of foods that are dangerous for your pet.

Serve up your pet's meals in a small ceramic dish that is too heavy for them to knock over. Do not expect the animals to neatly empty their dishes.

These two Campbell's Russian hamsters drink from the spout of a water bottle. Water bottles in many different sizes are sold in all pet stores.

Hamsters and gerbils like to hide bits of their food and dig them up later. Be sure to remove food that has been in the dish—or has been hidden—for too long. This is especially true for fresh fruits and vegetables that can spoil or rot.

Like all animals, hamsters and gerbils need fresh water to stay healthy. A hanging bottle with a sipping tube is the best way to give it to them. A water dish will get knocked over or filled with pieces of bedding.

Toys

Hamsters and gerbils need to play. It gives them exercise and keeps them healthy, happy, and interested in the world around them. Most hamsters and gerbils love to run on an exercise wheel. The safest kind of wheel is a solid-bottom one instead of a wire

Some wheels can be attached to the walls of a wire cage, while others can stand on their own anywhere in the cage.

31

wheel. When using wire wheels, your pet's small feet or tail can get caught in between the wires.

A wadded-up paper bag can also make a great toy. Your hamster can use it for bedding or as a hideout. A hollow wooden log with holes—made especially for hamsters or gerbils and sold at pet stores—will give them something to climb through for hours of fun. Using wooden ladders, ramps, and cardboard boxes, you can build a playground right inside your pet's cage.

These gerbils enjoy playing on and hiding inside these plastic cubes. Pet stores sell little houses for your pet in a variety of shapes, sizes, and colors.

Playing It Safe

Hamsters and gerbils are happy to play in their cages, but they enjoy exploring the bigger world, too. There are several safe ways to let your pet play outside its cage. No matter which ones you use, never leave your pet alone when it is outside of its cage.

Before you let your hamster or gerbil out of its cage, you will need to make sure the room is safe. Close the windows, doors, and any drawers. Remove any wires, cables, potted plants, and small open containers from the floor. Unplug electrical cords and cover up any pet-sized holes. Cover any heating or cooling vents located on the floor or low on the wall so that your pet will not accidentally fall in. If you have a cat or a dog, be sure to keep them out of the room while your hamster or gerbil is loose. Even if they get along most of the time, the larger animal can accidentally hurt your little rodent.

Many people prefer to let their pet use a special plastic ball made for hamsters or gerbils. The ball opens and closes to let the pet in or out. It also has special air holes so the animal can breathe. When your pet runs inside it, the ball will roll around the room. Just make sure it does not roll down a staircase!

Some stores sell special gerbil or hamster "playpens." This gives your pets space to roam safely, and you will not have to pet-proof an entire room. Another available playpen is a bathtub. Just be sure to rinse out any soap

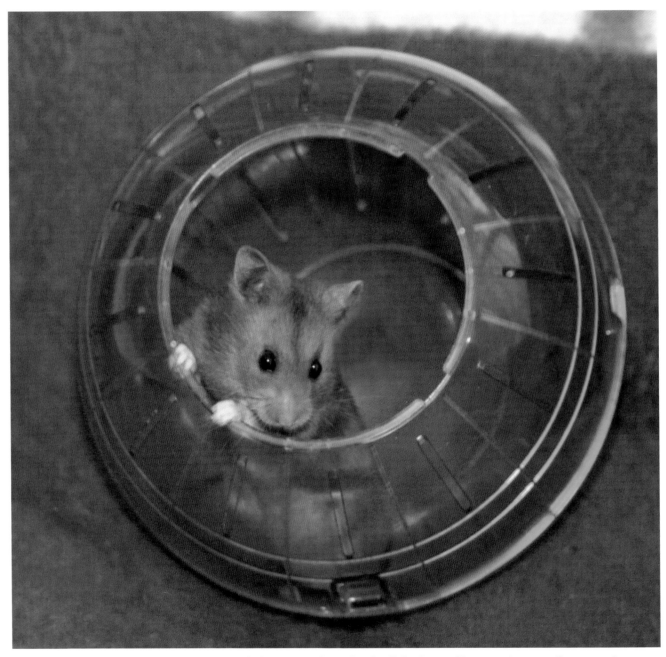

You should let your hamster or gerbil get used to the ball before allowing it to roll around. Though most pets enjoy this toy, some will not, and you should not force them to use it.

or chemicals and to cover up the drain before putting your pet inside. Add a couple of its toys and you can let your little friend run around inside the tub. The bathtub is also a good option because it is easy to clean after your pet goes back to its cage.

Cleaning House

Keeping your pet's home clean is very important, and not too hard to do. There are some tasks that should be done every day. These include rinsing and refilling the water bottle and looking for and throwing out pieces of fresh food your pet has hidden. Also, you should remove the dirty or soiled shavings and bedding if your pet has gone to the bathroom on them. Replace the shavings and bedding with fresh material.

A hamster cage should be cleaned every week. Gerbil cages can be cleaned once every two weeks. First, put your pet in a safe place where it cannot escape or hurt itself. Throw out all the shavings and hidden food. Take out any plastic or wooden toys, tubes, tunnels, or hiding places. These should be washed with hot water. You can use a mild soap, but be sure to rinse it off really well. Once it is empty, the cage or tank should also be scrubbed with hot water and mild soap. When the cage or tank is dry, replace the bedding and shavings and put the toys, tubes, water bottle, and food dish back in.

If your cage has many different parts and pieces—such as tunnels, houses, and wheels—you must be sure to wash everything when you clean the cage. A clean cage will help keep you and your pet healthy.

WARNING!

It is important to keep your pet's home clean, but it is also important for you to stay safe and healthy while caring for your pet. If you keep your pet in a glass aquarium or tank, have an adult help you clean it so that it does not accidentally break.

Never wash the cage or toys in your kitchen sink. The dirt and other wastes from the cage can make you sick if it gets into your dishes, food, or drinks. A bathtub is the perfect place to wash the cage and toys. Just be sure to clean the tub or sink with a disinfectant soap afterward. Also be sure to wash your hands and arms very well. You should always wash your hands after handling your pet or any of its food or supplies.

Getting to Know Your Pet

When you bring your new pet home, it will probably feel nervous. So it is a good idea to let it settle down and get used to its surroundings before you try to pick it up. If you talk to it softly whenever you are near its cage, it will start to recognize your voice. After a couple of days, rest your hand in its cage, palm up. Gerbils might run the first few times you do this. But they are very curious animals, and probably will not be able to resist coming over to

A HEALTHY PET

Hamsters and gerbils are hardy little animals, but they can sometimes become sick. Before you bring home your pet, find a **veterinarian,** or vet, with an office near your home. Not all vets treat small animals like hamsters and gerbils, so be sure to call first to make sure.A local breeder, shelter, or pet store can probably tell you which vets in your area handle hamsters and gerbils. You can also look in the telephone book or on the Internet for local vets who handle small animals.

Hopefully, you will never have to bring your pet to the vet. But if your hamster or gerbil looks ill, acts differently, or stops eating, drinking, or going to the bathroom, call the vet. You will probably have to bring your pet to be checked out and treated. Vets can also give you advice on proper pet care.

investigate and sniff. A hamster might take longer, but eventually it will want to explore, too. This is a good time to offer one of those sunflower seeds to help your pet overcome its shyness! After a few days, your pet will be used to your hand and come to it eagerly. Soon, you will be able to pick it up. Some hamsters and gerbils are ready to be held soon after coming home. It all depends on your pet's personality and nervousness.

Some hamsters and gerbils are very comfortable being held and snuggled right from the start. Others will need a little more time to get used to their new human friends.

Holding Your Pet

You must be careful when handling your pet. You should not reach for your pet from directly above. It might get scared of the large object coming down from above and run away or bite. Instead, slowly scoop up your pet from the sides.

Slowly offering treats and getting your hamster or gerbil used to your hands is the first step to learning to hold your pet.

Lift your pet gently and sit on the floor with it so it will not get hurt if it jumps or falls. Your gerbil might investigate your arm and climb all the way up to your shoulder. Your hamster might want to be cuddled close to your chest or check out one of your pockets to see if there is a tasty treat inside. The more time you spend holding and playing with your hamster or gerbil, the more it will get used to you.

Within a few weeks, your pets will know you and trust you. Inside or outside the cage, they will love being with you as much as you love being with them!

Hamsters and gerbils are great little pets that can bring a lot of love and happiness into your life.

Glossary

breeder—A person who breeds and raises animals.

burrow—A hole or nest that an animal digs in the ground. Can also be used as a verb that means "to dig."

descendant—The related offspring (or children) of a parent or grand parent. For example, you are a descendant of your great great grandparents.

gnaw—To chew or bite—pronounced like *naw*.

incisor—The strong teeth in the front of the mouth. Gerbils and hamsters use them to chew and bite.

pup—A baby hamster or gerbil.

predators—Animals that hunt other animals for food.

rodent—A type of small mammal, including hamsters and gerbils, with large front teeth that never stop growing.

species—A specific type of animal. For example, a Syrian hamster is a species of rodent.

veterinarian—A doctor who treats animals—often called a "vet" for short.

Find Out More

Books

Anastasi, Donna. *Gerbils: The Complete Guide to Gerbil Care*. Irvine, CA: Bowtie Press, 2005.

Guidry, Virginia Parker. *Hamsters: The Ultimate Pocket Pet*. Irvine, CA: Bowtie Press, 2004.

Kotter, Engelbert. *My Gerbil and Me*. Hauppauge, NY: Barron's Educational Series, 2002.

Richardson, Adele. *Caring for Your Hamster*. Mankato, MN: Capstone Press, 2007.

Sjonger, Rebecca and Bobbie Kalman. *Hamsters*. St. Catherine's, Ontario: Crabtree Publishing, 2004.

Web Sites

The American Gerbil Society

http://www.agsgerbils.org/index.php

This organization's Web site has information on gerbil care, gerbil shows, and names of breeders grouped by state and country to help you find one in your area.

A.S.P.C.A Animaland

http://www.aspca.org/site/PageServer?pagename=kids_pc_home

This Web site has a lot of kid-friendly tips on hamster and gerbil care.

The National Gerbil Society

http://www.gerbils.co.uk

The National Gerbil Society has information on gerbil care, plus fun gerbil wallpaper for your computer and nineteenth-century illustrations of gerbils.

The National Hamster Council

http://www.hamsters-uk.org

This organization is the oldest hamster club in the world. Its Web site offers fact sheets, articles, and information on all the varieties of pet hamsters.

Index

About the Author

Carol Ellis has written several books for young readers. She grew up with a variety of pets, including cats, dogs, parakeets, and tropical fish. She and her family live in New York, where they share their home with two cats.